Pemberville Public Library

RAPLB

880619

j394.2   Whitlock, Ralph
           Thanksgiving and
           harvest

Pemberville Public Library
375 E. Front St.
Pemberville, OH 43450

Holidays & Festivals
THANKSGIVING AND HARVEST

Ralph Whitlock

Rourke Enterprises, Inc.
Vero Beach, FL 32964

Holidays and Festivals

Buddhist Festivals
Christmas
Jewish Festivals
Muslim Festivals
New Year
Thanksgiving and Harvest

First published in the United States in 1987
by Rourke Enterprises Inc., Vero Beach, FL 32964

Text © 1987 Rourke Enterprises, Inc.

All rights reserved. No part of this book may be reproduced or utilized in any form or by any means, electronic or mechanical including photocopying, recording or by any information storage and retrieval system without permission in writing from the publisher.

Library of Congress Cataloging-in-Publication Data

Whitlock, Ralph.
    Thanksgiving and harvest.

    (Holiday and festivals)
    Bibliography: p.
    Includes index.
    Summary: Describes the origins and traditions of harvest festivals and Thanksgiving celebrations around the world.
    1. Harvest festivals – Juvenile literature.
2. Thanksgiving Day - Juvenile literature.
[1. Harvest festivals.   2. Thanksgiving Day]
I. Title.   II. Series: Holidays and festivals.
GT4380.W44   1987   394.2'683   87–4282

ISBN 0–86592–976–9

Phototypeset by The Grange Press, Southwick, Sussex
Printed in Italy by G. Canale & C.S.p.A., Turin

Contents

Why Have a Harvest Festival? 4

Harvests around the World 6

Harvests in Other Times and Places 10

Celebrating the Harvest in Britain
Harvest Festivals 14
When Everybody Helped with the Harvest 16
The End of the Harvest 18
The Gleaners 20
The Corn Dolly 22

Thanksgiving in North America
The First Thanksgiving 24
Thanksgiving Day 26

Harvest Festivals around the World
Australia, Oceania and the Far East 28
India and Africa 32

The Festival of the First Fruits 34

The Jewish Feast of Pentecost 36

Traditional Harvests
Forest Harvests 38
The Harvest of Animals 40
The Harvest of the Sea 42

Tomorrow's Harvest Festival 44

Glossary 46
Further Reading 46
Index 47

Why Have a Harvest Festival?

A harvest scene of two hundred years ago.

Until a few hundred years ago, most people had only the food they produced for themselves. Most of them lived in villages and worked on farms. In the fields, they grew wheat and barley, sometimes oats. They kept cows, sheep, pigs, goats, poultry and bees. The cows gave them milk and meat, and did much of the farm work. The sheep gave wool, as well as milk and meat. Some of the fields around a village were reserved for grazing by the

Today, not many people rely on the food that they grow themselves to survive.

farm animals, or were cut for hay as their winter food. Pigs could get most of their food in the woods. They were very fond of acorns, so when the oak trees bore lots of acorns, the people spoke of "a good acorn harvest." It was important to them. Acorns and hazelnuts were used for grinding into flour, and mixing with wheat flour to make bread in times of scarcity.

In the past, the farmers had poor-quality seeds and did not fully understand the need for fertilizing the soil by manuring, so they often had poor harvests. When a drought prevented the crops from growing, or when wet weather interfered with the harvesting, the harvests were very poor, indeed. Many farm animals died from diseases that would now be easily cured. When these disasters occurred, there were no stores or supermarkets to which the people could go to buy food. So they had to go without. In the records of those days, a phrase that often appears is: "A year of famine." In such a year, many people and animals starved.

So when the farms had good harvests, and when the farm animals produced many healthy young, everyone was delighted. When all the grain had been harvested and the hay had been stored in the barns, it was the time for everyone to have a merry feast. They knew that they had a good chance of surviving another year.

Harvests around the World

Combine harvesters on a wheat farm in Kansas.

Every day of the year, a harvest is being gathered somewhere in the world. In countries in the northern hemisphere, harvests ripen in the summer, which is from June to September. Wheat, for instance, which is one of the chief harvests, is sown in the fields in the previous autumn or in spring, and grows all through the warm months until, in late summer, the grain is ripe. Then the wheat is harvested, made into flour, and used to make bread.

In the southern hemisphere, June to September is wintertime. There, the summer comes between

In Greece, the grape harvest occurs in November.

December and March. But the sequence of events is the same. In many parts of the tropics, the year is divided between wet seasons and dry seasons. Seeds are sown or plants are planted in the wet season, and the crops are harvested early in the dry season. In parts of the tropics that have no long periods of drought, crops may be grown and harvested all year round. Farmers can take as many as four harvests a year from the same plot of land. In desert and semi-desert countries, farmers can achieve the same results by using irrigation.

In countries in the northern hemisphere, the harvest travels northward as the summer progresses. In North America, for instance, a contractor with a combine harvester will begin harvesting grain in Texas in June and, moving northward as the harvest ripens, will finish up harvesting in Canada in October. In Europe, grain harvests have ended in the Mediterranean countries before they have started in Scandinavia and Britain.

Grain harvests are, of course, not the only harvests. In Britain, one of the first harvests of the year is the strawberry harvest, which starts in June, and one of the latest is the potato harvest, which sometimes does not finish until November. In France and West Germany, one of the late autumn harvests is grapes.

Some crops can be harvested very quickly. If you sow mustard and cress seeds in a saucer and cut it for salad three weeks later, you have achieved a harvest within three weeks. Cutting trees, too, when they have reached their prime can be termed harvesting, but the trees may then be eighty years or more old.

In the tropics, the crops that can be grown and harvested three or four times a year on the same land, are mostly tall, quick-growing plants, which are used for feeding farm animals. Corn, cut when green, and kale are examples. Allowing cows or sheep to graze grass is really a method of harvesting the grass. Harvests are not even necessarily of food crops. Cotton, for instance, is a crop that

Spanish farmers collecting stalks of corn after harvesting.

Today, we can buy the food we need. Two hundred years ago, many people relied on the food that they grew themselves.

produces an annual harvest, but its harvest is of the soft, white fiber that covers the seeds and is used for weaving into fabrics.

The harder it is to produce a harvest and the longer it takes, the greater the feeling of pleasure and achievement when the harvest is successfully gathered. That is why harvest festivals have evolved and become popular chiefly in countries with temperate climates. The grain harvest in those countries comes only once a year, and is often the climax of a whole year of effort. All countries have festivals, but not all festivals are associated with harvests.

Harvests in Other Times and Places

Wherever people have had to produce their own food, they have always felt the same about the harvest – as if they have won enough money in a lottery to last them for a whole year. Of course, winning money in a lottery is pure luck, whereas people who grow food have to work hard for it. But still there is an element of luck about it. A long drought starving the crops of water in the middle of the growing season, or a torrential thunder-storm just as the wheat is ripe, can ruin what might otherwise be a good harvest.

Food growers have always wondered, too, about the life in the seed they sowed. How did it come there, and what made it grow and develop? They realized that when they had done everything they could, there were still things quite outside their control, such as bad weather, disease and this mysterious life force, which could make the difference between success and failure. To them, such matters were supernatural. So when they held a festival to celebrate a good harvest, they were always careful to give thanks to the unseen powers on which they obviously had to rely. All harvest festivals, in every age and place, are

Ceres, the Greek goddess of agriculture.

occasions for thanksgiving to the gods.

Combined with this feeling was the belief that efforts should be made to ensure that the god would be equally helpful the following year. The matter was clearly urgent because, after harvest in the northern hemisphere, the days were growing shorter, the sun was lower in the sky at midday, and the weather was becoming colder. What if the cycle of the seasons failed? What if the sun never ceased its decline and vanished altogether? So in celebrating a successful harvest, the people of many countries in ancient times devised prayers and rituals to keep the harvest gods happy. And

An Egyptian tomb painting of workers gathering in the grain harvest.

A sixteenth-century drawing of an Inca harvest-time ceremony.

they invented stories to explain what the gods were doing.

Among the Greeks and Romans, the goddess of agriculture was Ceres. Her festival, which lasted for eight days, was called Cerealia, from which our word "cereal" is derived. Ceres' daughter, Proserpine, was carried off by Pluto to be Queen of the Underworld but, after a lot of trouble, a compromise was arranged whereby Proserpine spent six months of every year on earth with her parents, and six months down in the Underworld with Pluto. The six months when she was absent were winter, and her six months on earth were summer. Her return was celebrated with great rejoicing.

In Egypt, the season of renewal and the arrival of the Nile floods were said to be due to the arrival of the god Osiris. He had been killed and chopped to pieces by his enemies, but was restored to life every year at a set time.

On the other side of the world, American Indians observed similar festivals. The rain god of the Central American Mayas, for instance, brought water for the crops, and the sun god provided warmth and light. Ceremonies in their honor were day-long affairs, with much dancing, and usually with a play about the revival of nature. In South America, the Incas had a harvest festival called the Great Cultivation at the time of the corn harvest. Llamas were sacrificed to the sun god, and lavish feasts were enjoyed. Two

months earlier, the festival of Earth Ripening was an anxious occasion, accompanied by a fast rather than a feast, as the people invited the sun god's aid in helping the harvest to ripen. Some of the Indian tribes of North America also had a day of mourning when they cut the first corn. The purpose of their mourning was to show the corn goddess how sorry they were to have to help themselves to her property.

Similar festivals are to be found in the customs of almost all ancient peoples.

North American Indians tilling the land and planting seeds.

Celebrating the Harvest in Britain

Brightly colored costumes are worn at large harvest fairs in Russia.

Harvest Festivals

In Britain, harvest festivals are celebrated in churches and Sunday schools. The church is beautifully decorated with flowers, greenery and fruit. In the front of the church, around the altar or pulpit, are gifts of more flowers, fruit and vegetables brought by the congregation. Everyone brings the biggest and best products they have grown in their gardens. There are huge

British churches are decorated with flowers, greenery and fruit for the harvest festival.

marrows, bright red apples, snow-white cauliflowers, bunches of grapes and, if it can be obtained, a sheaf of wheat. The local baker often brings a big loaf made in the shape of a wheat sheaf.

During the morning service, the children bring their gifts. They assemble in the porch, and walk in procession up the aisle to present them to the clergyman. They, too, will have flowers, fruit and vegetables from their gardens, and also things they have bought, such as eggs, jars of jam, oranges and cans of fruit. All their gifts are placed on a special table, and the clergyman offers a prayer of blessing for them. In the service that follows, special harvest hymns, such as "Come, Ye Thankful People, Come" and "We Plow the Fields" are sung. The church is usually full for harvest festivals.

The idea is to present to God a sample of the harvests for which the people have worked all the year. Nowadays, though, not many people have to rely on the food that they themselves grow. They make their living by working at other jobs and buy their food with the money they earn. So they buy many of the things they take to the harvest festival, though they still like to offer the produce from their gardens. In most churches, too, a lump of coal and a glass of water will be displayed with the other gifts, to show that these also are regarded as gifts from God. And men and women who are good at crafts often bring along some samples of their work.

15

When Everybody Helped with the Harvest

The wheat harvest is ready about six weeks after the wheat plant comes into flower. In Britain, northern Europe and much of America, that is around the end of July. The farmer decides when the wheat is to be cut. Before harvesting was mechanized, it was cut either by sickle or by scythe. When the wheat was cut by sickle, the reaper grasped the ears of wheat with one hand, and cut them off a few inches from the top. The stalks, or straw, were cut separately. When using a scythe, the reaper cut the wheat plant just above ground level. His wife, following behind, gathered up the fallen stalks and tied them into sheaves, using twisted straw for tying.

Other men and women picked up the sheaves and stood them in tent-shaped clumps, known as stooks or hiles, for drying. The drying took a week or two if the weather remained fine, but

Farm workers wielding their scythes at harvest time.

A Dakota wheat farm about a hundred years ago.

longer if there were rainstorms. As soon as the sheaves were dry, they were collected on wagons and taken to the farmyard or a corner of the field. There they were built into stacks or ricks. Later on, in winter, they were pulled apart and threshed, to separate the grain from the straw. The grain was ground into flour and made into bread. But the harvest was considered finished when the last wagon-load was built into a rick.

There were so many things to be done in the harvest field that everyone living nearby was required to help. Even the children were kept busy. Some led the horses that pulled the wagons. Some helped to stand the sheaves into hiles. Some helped their mothers bind the sheaves. Everyone worked all day long, and sometimes by moonlight, too. The harvest usually lasted six weeks, but longer if it rained. No wonder everyone felt very pleased and thankful when the last sheaf was finally collected.

The End of the Harvest

Each farm in a village tried hard to finish its harvest first. The farmworkers wanted to get the grain safely stored before it rained, of course, but also they liked to score over their neighbors. When the last sheaf was picked up from the stubble, one of the men hoisted it on his prong and raised the "harvest shout":

> Well plowed!
> Well sowed!
> Well harrowed!
> Well mowed!
> And all safely carted to the barn with never a load throwed!
> Hip, hip, hooray!

A harvest-home song that was sung as the last wagon-load traveled homeward.

All the harvesters joined in the shout, which echoed across the fields, letting workers on the other farms know that this farm had finished its harvest.

As the last wagon-load trundled homeward, the horses were adorned with ribbons and rosettes, and the wagon with green boughs. If possible, everyone who had helped with the harvest clambered on the wagon, shouting and singing as they made their way home. Sometimes they paraded all around the village, calling at the public houses for a drink.

The next evening, a "harvest-home feast" was laid on trestle tables in the great barn. The menu generally consisted of boiled beef or mutton with carrots, potatoes, cabbage and dumplings, followed by plum pudding. Sometimes there were hams, rabbits, chicken, hares, cheese and cake. For drink they had plenty of ale or cider. After the meal was finished, speeches were made, toasts were drunk, and songs were sung. Later, the harvesters danced to violin or accordion music.

An important person in the harvest field was the Lord of the Harvest. It was he who organized the workers, allotting each one his task. Wielding his scythe, he set the pace for the reapers, and when the sheaves were being carted, if was often he who built the rick. He drove the last wagon home, and sat next to the farmer at the harvest-home feast.

Dancing at the harvest-home feast.

The Gleaners

Old-time harvest-home suppers sometimes had a Harvest Queen. She was not elected for the occasion, and was not necessarily a pretty girl. Usually, she was the wife or girlfriend of the Lord of the Harvest. When he was mowing with the scythe, she tied the sheaves for him. Later she was in charge of any women who were arranging the sheaves in hiles.

As soon as a field was cleared of sheaves, she led the women in to begin gleaning. Gleaning is a very ancient custom, described in the Bible. In the

A gleaner with her sickle and a sheaf of grain.

A 1950s photograph of farm-workers building a rick.

Book of Leviticus, the farmer is commanded to leave the gleanings for "the stranger, the fatherless and the widow." Gleaning means picking up the stray ears of wheat or other grain that are left in the field after the sheaves are gathered.

The women and children used to do the gleaning, picking up the ears by hand and putting them into burlap bags hanging from their waists. A poor woman could sometimes collect enough grain to provide her and her family with bread for much of the winter. Each day she would carry home all the ears she had collected, and store them in a sack in the kitchen. After the harvest, she rubbed the grain out of the ears, and took it to the miller who ground in into flour. At home she would knead it into dough, and bake it in her oven.

Only wheat was gleaned. Sheep were allowed to forage in oat fields after the harvest, and pigs fed in the barley stubble. But in Mediterranean countries, gleaners were allowed to gather grapes.

The Corn Dolly

Corn dollies are now purely ornamental, although they used to be an important part of the harvest. In Britain, "corn" refers to any kind of grain.

Corn dollies are made of straw. In the past, they were made from the last straw to be cut, since the harvesters believed that that was where the "corn goddess" was living.

Corn dollies like this one were once an important part of the harvest.

We have already learned how the harvesters were careful to thank the goddess who gave life to the seed and caused it to grow. They thought that she lived in the soil, but when the soil started to produce crops of wheat, barley and other plants, she moved up to live in them. When the harvesters started to cut the grain, they believed they were robbing her of her home. When they came to the end of the harvest, they thought that she must

The last sheaf of the harvest is held aloft in this 1954 picture of a field at harvest time.

be in the few stalks that were left. So the reapers very reverently approached those stalks, with their caps pulled down over their faces, so that the goddess would not be able to recognize the man who made the last cut.

When the last stalks were severed, they were carefully collected and handed to a skillful weaver. With them he made an image of the corn goddess. She was carried in triumph to the barn for the harvest-home feast, where she was set at the head of the table. Toasts were drunk to her, and songs praising her were sung. For the rest of the winter, she stood on the mantelshelf in the farmhouse hall. People treated her with respect, because they believed she must not be offended.

When plowing began in January, she was carried back to the fields and there laid gently in the first furrow. The plow turned the soft, brown earth on top of her. She was now safely buried in the soil again, ready to perform the usual miracle and produce another harvest. Nearly every European country knows about the corn goddess and makes straw images of her.

Thanksgiving in North America

The First Thanksgiving

Thanksgiving Day in the United States started with the Pilgrim Fathers, who sailed from England in the *Mayflower* to escape from religious persecution. Because of delays in starting, the ship did not arrive in America until November 10, when it was too late to sow crops that year. So for the first winter, they had to rely on the remains of the food they had brought with them, and whatever animals and birds they could catch. Fortunately, the local Indians were friendly and brought them food, otherwise probably none of them would have survived. As it was, nearly half of the 100 or so settlers died.

In the spring, however, they cleared land, cultivated it and grew successful crops of grain. By July, it was clear that they were going to have a harvest big enough to see them through the next winter. So the governor of the little colony announced that they would have a three-day festival of thanksgiving. One of the days would also be a day of prayer and would be known as Thanksgiving Day. It was July 30 in the year 1621.

They spent days preparing for the feast. The men caught fish and snared geese and ducks. The Indians, who also joined in, brought carcasses of

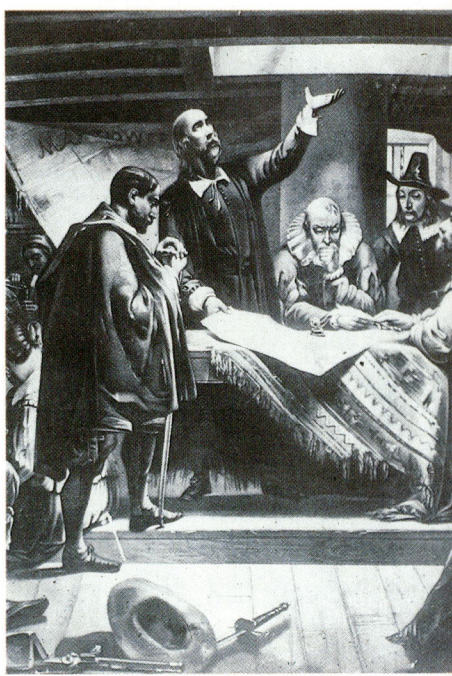

The Pilgrim Fathers on the Mayflower, *leaving England for America.*

24

A Thanksgiving dinner among the Puritans.

deer and wild turkeys. The women and children gathered nuts, which they ground up and mixed with cornmeal to make bread. They also found wild plums, grapes and watercress. Then the women roasted the meat over fires in the open air, and cooked green corn, beans and leeks. And on Thanksgiving Day they all sat outdoors at big tables and ate their feast and thanked God for the harvest.

This happened at Plymouth, Massachusetts, where the Pilgrims landed. Later, as other settlers arrived on the New England coast, they heard of the Thanksgiving Day celebration at Plymouth, and thought it was a good idea. And so the custom spread throughout the colonies.

A family enjoying a Thanksgiving dinner.

Thanksgiving Day

In the 150 years after the Pilgrim Fathers celebrated the first Thanksgiving Day at Plymouth, Massachusetts, the festival became generally observed all along the eastern coast of America. And when, at the time of the War of Independence, the Americans wanted to celebrate their victories, they did it on Thanksgiving Day. In 1789, George Washington decreed that Thanksgiving Day should be officially kept on November 26 every year.

Since then, the date has been changed several times, the latest being as recently as 1941. Now it is the fourth Thursday of November, which is a national holiday all over the United States. Canada also has a Thanksgiving Day, but it is on a different date. Since 1957 it has been the second Monday of October.

Football has become very much a part of Thanksgiving.

In both countries, Thanksgiving Day is kept in the same way. It is a happy occasion when members of a family like to get together and share a big meal. The traditional Thanksgiving Day dish is roast turkey with cranberry sauce and pumpkin pie, but the table is loaded with all kinds of other goodies, most of them homemade. The theme is thankfulness for peace and plenty, and the happiness of family life during the past year. Some people attend Thanksgiving services in church, and for many, watching the Macy's Thanksgiving Day parade on television has become a tradition.

Many people simply enjoy the occasion without thinking much about what it means or how it came about. It is a good opportunity for a long holiday weekend and marks the beginning of the Christmas shopping season.

Harvest Festivals around the World

Australia, Oceania and the Far East

In Australia and New Zealand, people have harvest festivals that are much the same as in Britain, the country from which most of the settlers came. Harvest festivals are church festivals, to which people bring their gifts of flowers, fruit, vegetables and other produce. People sing the same hymns of thanksgiving and listen to sermons on the same theme. The chief difference is that they are held on different dates from those in Europe and America. The wheat is harvested in February and March instead of in August and September, and the festival is naturally held when the harvest is finished.

In Australia, wheat, barley and oats are still the crops most widely grown, but as the tropical parts of the continent are developed, so tropical plants, especially sugarcane, are becoming important. Farm animals are, however, the most important agricultural product of Australia. Vast numbers of sheep are kept for their meat and their wool,

In Australia, sugarcane is becoming an important crop.

and on the great farms of the outback, the sheep-shearing is often the occasion for a festival. New Zealand, too, relies more on its farm animals than its crops, but here dairy cows are as important as sheep. The islands of Oceania, of which one of the biggest if Fiji, are mostly tropical, and so grow such crops as coconuts, bananas, rice and yams, as well as sugarcane. Because most of the inhabitants are Christian, they have similar harvest festivals to those of Britain and America.

Shearing sheep on a farm in the Australian outback.

Ceremonial dancers at a Japanese autumn thanksgiving festival.

Japan, being on the same latitude as Britain and much of America, grows similar crops, and also rice, and harvests them at about the same time. Japan has an important autumn festival called the New Taste Festival, because in old times rice from the new harvest was not supposed to be eaten until the festival had been held. Just as the peasants of old Europe honored a corn goddess, so the Japanese honor a rice spirit. On festival days, she is supposed to ride in a sacred cart, leading a procession of worshipers who dance and sing and wave torches and fans. Either before or afterward, everyone sits down to a grand feast, with lots of rice wine to drink.

The New Taste Festival has now been officially fixed on November 23 as a national holiday, and is called Labor Thanksgiving Day. In a solemn thanksgiving ritual at midnight, the Emperor of Japan presents the first fruits of the harvest at a special altar. So, on behalf of his people, he identifies himself with the mysterious spirit that gives life to the harvest.

The Autumn Festival in China was not so closely related to the harvest. It was certainly an occasion for a feast, but it was chiefly in honor of the moon. Women used to climb to the tops of pagodas to be as near to the moon as possible, and while there they made secret wishes.

In the eastern countries where the Buddha is worshiped, which include Sri Lanka, Burma and Vietnam, a great festival is held at the first full moon after the rainy season ends. The peasant farmers bring gifts to the Buddhist monks and to the poor. Every house and temple is decorated with flowers, and brightly lit with colored lights. The festival is said to commemorate the return of the Buddha to this earth.

Balinese women taking offerings to a temple.

India and Africa

India and Africa are both lands with large numbers of peasant farmers, who are well aware of their dependence on their crops, and on the gods or spirits who help to produce them. Most religions in both India and Africa have thanksgiving festivals for good harvests.

Some African tribes at harvest time present the "first fruits" to the gods, or to the spirits of the tribal ancestors. Then the people eat any food that remains from last year's harvest. Only after that can they taste the first of the new harvest.

In some Arab countries, the harvesters have a ceremony very similar to that of the old corn dolly tradition in Europe. When they cut the last handful of wheat stalks, the harvesters tie them into a sheaf and lay it in an open grave. They mark the head and the foot of the grave with stones. Then they cover the sheaf with soil and the chief utters a prayer, "May Allah give us back the wheat from the dead."

Part of an Indian thanksgiving festival celebrating a good harvest.

Nigerian women buying bananas in a food market.

In northern India and in other eastern countries, ceremonies are held at the end of the harvest to drive away any devils that may have got into the granaries. A priest takes a little cart around the village, and from every house collects a little grain. This is taken to wasteland beyond the edge of the village fields, and thrown away by young men who beat it, and each other, with sticks. The grain is for the spirits who, it is hoped, will be content with their share.

Christian congregations in Africa and India have adopted harvest festivals, as well as many other festivals, in the Christian calendar. Many African Christians set aside a plot of land, which they call God's acre, for growing crops for their church. When the crops are harvested, they are sold at a harvest festival, and the money is given to the church or to some charity.

33

The Festival of the First Fruits

Most harvest festivals are celebrated at the end of the harvest, but some were held at the beginning. In some Christian countries, when the grain was ripe and ready for harvesting, people felt that they should give God thanks for providing their food for another year. So they then held a thanksgiving festival, called the Festival of the First Fruits, before gathering the crops.

Detail instructions about the Festival of the First Fruits are found in Chapter 26 of the Book of Deuteronomy. The farmer is told to take the first fruits of his harvest, which means the first wheat and barley as well as the first grapes and plums, and put them in a basket. He must then take them to the priest and present them to him with certain set words of thanks.

When England became Christian, hundreds of years ago, the people followed these instructions and added to them. Instead of taking the first ears of wheat to the priest, they first ground them into flour. With the flour they made little round loaves of bread, and these they brought to church for the priest to bless. So the festival became known as Loaf-mass, "mass" being a word then meaning a festival or a celebration. As the years went by, people slurred "Loaf-mass," and spoke of "Lammas." Lammastide was August 1, which eventually became August Bank Holiday in England. So when, in 1965 the government moved August Bank Holiday from the beginning to the end of August, it interfered with a very old custom, indeed.

An English harvest festival service of about 70 years ago.

Left *Presenting the small loaves of bread to the priest at the celebration of Loaf-mass.*

The Jewish Feast of Pentecost

The calendar of the Jewish religion has two harvest festivals, one celebrating the gathering of the early wheat harvest, the other the gathering of fruit. The first is known as the Feast of Pentecost. Pentecost is a word meaning "fiftieth," the feast being held on the fiftieth day after the great Feast of the Passover. At services in synagogues on that day, readings are given from the Book of Ruth, which is a story of events on a farm in Palestine "in the time of barley harvest," long ago. The synagogues are specially decorated with flowers and plants for the occasion, and a family feast is held.

The festival of the fruit harvest is the Feast of Tabernacles, or Succoth. The Sukkah, from which the name Succoth is taken, is a kind of tent or hut with an open roof. Here a Jewish family eats its meals and sometimes sleeps during the week of the festival. It is a reminder of the days, long ago, when people used to live in tents and temporary huts when they were away from home, gathering fruit. As the festival occurs in the autumn, when food is abundant, the meals each day are real feasts. There is plenty of everything, but especially of fruit. The family takes a long time over the meals, saying thanksgiving prayers and graces and blessing the fruit, the tent, the wine and everything. The tents are decorated

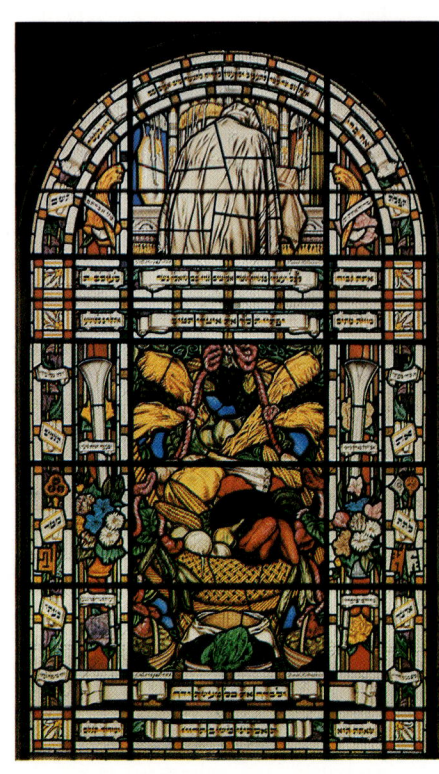

A synagogue stained-glass window showing the flowers, fruit and produce of the field.

A Jewish family celebrating the Succoth in a Sukkah.

with flowers, fruit and greenery, and lit by colored lights. The synagogues are also gaily decorated. Every day there are processions, when the people carry palm branches and sing hymns. On the seventh day, there is a specially long procession and ceremony, after which the tents and all the decorations are taken down.

Both festivals began very early in Jewish history, when the Jews were farming people. For Christians, the Feast of Pentecost has become Whitsuntide, when the Holy Spirit was given to the world.

Traditional Harvests

Forest Harvests

Forests once covered a far greater area of most countries than they do now. They have been cleared to make room for farmland and buildings. In times past, the harvests the forests produced were quite important. The harvests included nuts, acorns, berries, roots and fungi, as well as the trees themselves, the undergrowth and the bracken.

In autumn, whole families went gathering nuts and acorns in the woods. Often they took picnics and even camped out overnight. Both the nuts

A Victorian family gathering acorns in the woods.

and the acorns were shelled, pounded into flour and mixed with wheat flour to make bread. In many countries, pigs were turned loose in the woods to feed on acorns, which they like very much. Women used to dig up the roots of certain plants that were used as medicine, and they picked wild blackberries, raspberries, strawberries and other berries for making desserts and jellies. Today, we do not put much value on acorns or roots, but we still go into the woods to pick nuts and berries.

In the days when the forest harvests were important for the winter food supply, they were celebrated with feasts and merrymaking. Often it was the custom to eat special dishes on these occasions – pigs' heads and apple dumplings, for example. Because the harvests were gathered in the autumn, the feasts became associated with saints whose feast days were fixed at that time in the Christian calendar. The most important of these saints was St. Michael, whose feast day, Michaelmas, is on September 29.

It is still popular to go into the countryside and collect berries and nuts.

The Harvest of Animals

Every year, the fields produced a crop of grain and the fruit trees produced a crop of fruit, and every year the farm animals produced a crop of young ones. The cows gave birth to calves, usually only one each. The ewes produced lambs, often twins. The sows produced two or more litters, each litter consisting of eight to twelve piglets. The hens hatched scores of chicks.

Large fairs, like this sheep fair, are a thing of the past.

In autumn, the villagers took stock of their animal harvest. They had to keep enough breeding animals to produce another crop of young ones next year, and others to provide meat for the families in the coming winter. The rest were surplus. Since there would not be enough food to keep all of them through the winter, some were sold or exchanged for goods, often at large gatherings called fairs. The St. Giles Fair at Winchester, one of the four great fairs of England in the Middle Ages, went on for sixteen days!

The animals that had been set aside for meat during the winter were killed in a great massacre in November. St. Martin's Day, November 11, known as Martinmas, was the date usually chosen. It was a local event, but everyone in the village was there. Great fires were lit, and everyone feasted on fresh meat. The rest of the animal carcasses were salted down for winter use.

Sheep, of course, produced another crop as well, wool. When they were sheared in early summer, the families of several farms met together to share the work and also to have a feast. While the men were shearing, the women prepared the feast, often cooking several sheep at a time.

Today, most farmers sell their animals through livestock auction markets, or have contracts to supply meat-processing plants. So fairs like the St. Giles Fair are now a thing of the past.

A prize bull at a New Zealand agricultural show.

The Harvest of the Sea

People who lived by the sea enjoyed a different type of harvest. They could add to their food supplies by catching fish. Fishermen soon learned that many fish arrived in shoals at certain seasons. Around Britain and in the seas of northern Europe, the main fishing season was between May and October. As the second part of it came at the same time as the grain harvest, often the women had to deal with the grain harvest while the men went fishing. While all this was going on, there was no time for festivals, especially as the fish had to be salted when they were brought home.

In the Shetland Isles, however, deep-sea fishing end at Lammastide – August 1 – and

This trawler crew are unloading their catch of cod from the North Sea.

A priest blessing the fishing fleet before it leaves port.

when all the boats were safely home a feast was held. All the fishermen and their wives sat down to a good meal, and then spent the evening telling stories, singing and drinking toasts. In the Isle of Man, the herring fishing season ended much later, and the fisherman's harvest festival, or "boat supper," was held on December 26. It was much the same as the feast held by the Shetland Islanders, but sometimes included a play about fishing adventures.

In many countries, the fishing boats are blessed by a priest before setting out to sea, and in some countries the fishermen kneel down on the decks of their boats to pray every evening. Fishing is a risky business, for sudden storms can blow up at sea, putting ships in danger. When the harvest of the sea is good, the fishermen and their families live well, but in times past when it failed, they sometimes starved.

Today, at Christian harvest festivals in churches in fishing ports, freshly caught fish and fishermen's nets are often displayed with the flowers, fruit and vegetables. One of the favorite hymns sung at harvest festivals is the "Manx Fishermen's Hymn." One verse reads:

> Our wives and children we commend to Thee;
> For them we plow the land and plow the deep;
> For them by day the golden corn we reap,
> By night the silver harvest of the sea.

Tomorrow's Harvest Festival

If we visit a harvest field next summer, we shall not find it crowded with people as it used to be. There will be one man on a combine harvester and another with a tractor and trailer, taking the grain back to the barn. That will be all. Only a very few people now earn their living from farming. Machines do most of the work.

Most of us do not have to grow our own food or look after farm animals. Instead, we buy what we need from a store or supermarket. Do you like to drink tea? The tea was probably grown by people in Sri Lanka, India or China. Do you like sugar with your tea? Much of it comes from Jamaica or Mauritius, or some other tropical country. Milk, butter and cheese come from cows, which most likely live in your state or a nearby one, especially if you live in the Midwest. And the wheat from which your bread, cookies and cakes are made was probably grown by farmers in the United States or Canada.

Our ancestors held their thanksgiving festival for the harvests of their own fields. Today, we celebrate the harvests of the whole world. And our thanks are due not only to the people who grow and harvest the food, but also to the people who bring it to us by land, sea or air. Harvest festivals have always been occasions when people

Machines now do all the work at harvest time.

Folk dancers at a Russian harvest fair.

have been proud and pleased with what they have achieved. That used to be mostly food, but now there are many other things that we can be proud and pleased about as well.

At harvest festivals, people have always brought samples of what they have been producing. It used to be sheaves of grain, or bunches of grapes, or something else from the fields and gardens. Today, in some countries people are beginning to bring samples of other things at which they have been working. They are thanking God for giving them the skill and patience and opportunity to produce them. That is just what their ancestors did with their sheaves of grain and their little loaves.

Glossary

Combine harvester A machine for cutting and threshing grain.
Congregation People gathered together for workship, usually in a church.
Contractor A person who agrees to do something at an arranged price.
Drought A serious lack of rain or water.
Famine A severe shortage of food.
Gleaning Gathering by hand stray ears of grain after the harvest.
Granaries Storehouses for grain.
Hiles Groups of sheaves stood up, tent fashion, to dry.
Reaper A person who cuts and gathers in crops of grain.
Rick A large stack of hay.
Scythe A large, curved blade on a long handle, used for cutting hay or grass by hand.
Sheaf A bundle of reaped grain tied together.
Sickle A tool with a curved blade and a short handle, used to cut grain or grass by hand.
Stubble The stubs or short ends of stalks left in the ground after the grain has been cut.
Synagogue A Jewish place of workship.
Temperate Moderate or mild in temperature.

Further reading

The First Thanksgiving Feast by Joan Anderson (Clarion, 1984)
Thanksgiving by Margaret Baldwin (Watts, 1983)
Turkeys, Pilgrims, and Indian Corn by Edna Barth (Clarion, 1975)
Thanksgiving Fun by Judith Corwin (Messner, 1984)
The Plymouth Thanksgiving by Leonard Weisgard (Doubleday, 1967)

For older readers:
Thanksgiving: An American Holiday, An American History by Diana Karter Appelbaum (Facts on File, 1984)

© Copyright 1984 Wayland (Publishers) Limited
61 Western Road, Hove, East Sussex BN3 1JD, England

Index

Acorns 5, 38, 39
Africa 32, 33
Agricultural produce
  butter 44
  cotton 8-9
  fruit *see* Fruit
  grain *see* Grain
  meat 4, 28, 41
  milk 4, 44
  rice 29, 30
  sugar 28, 29, 44
  tea 44
  wool 4, 28, 41
American Indians 12, 13
Arab countries 32
Australia 28-9

Bees 4
Bread 5, 6, 17, 21, 39
Britain 7, 8, 14-15, 16, 28, 30, 35, 42

Canada 7, 26, 44
  Thanksgiving *see* Thanksgiving
China 31, 44
Coconuts 29
Combine harvester 7, 44
Corn dolly 22-3, 32

Egypt 12
Europe 7, 16, 23, 28, 30, 32, 42

Fairs 41
  St. Giles Fair 41
Famine 5, 43
Farm animals 4, 5, 8, 28, 29, 40-41, 44
  cows 4, 8, 29, 40, 44
  goats 4
  poultry 4, 40
  sheep 4, 8, 21, 28, 29, 40
Fiji 29
Fish 24, 42-3
Flour 5, 6, 17, 21, 39
France 8
Fruit 28, 29, 36, 40
  bananas 29
  berries 38, 39
  grapes 8, 21, 35, 44
  strawberries 8

Grain 7, 9, 17, 18, 21, 22, 24, 33, 35, 40, 42, 44, 45
  barley 4, 21, 28, 35, 36
  corn 8, 12, 25
  oats 4, 21, 28
  wheat 4, 5, 10, 16, 21, 28, 32, 35, 36, 44
Growing season 6, 7, 10

Harvest
  and climate 7, 8, 9, 28, 29
  importance of 4-5, 10
  in northern hemisphere 6-7
  in southern hemisphere 6-7
Harvest festivals 5, 9, 10, 11, 12, 14-15, 18-19, 24, 25, 28, 29, 30-31, 32, 33, 35, 36-7, 39, 41, 42, 43, 44, 45
  church festivals 14-15, 27, 28, 33, 35, 43
  dancing 19, 31
  feasting 5, 12, 19, 23, 24-5, 31, 36, 39, 41, 43

Feast of Pentecost 36-7
First Fruits 34-5, 36
fisherman's 43
Great Cultivation 12
Lammas 35, 42
New Taste Festival 30-31
Succoth 36-7
Harvest gods 10, 11, 12, 13, 32, 33
Harvest hymns 15, 28, 43
Hay 5
Hiles *see* Stooks

India 32, 33, 44

Jamaica 44
Japan 30-31

New Zealand 28, 29

Oceania 13

Sheaves 16, 17, 18, 19, 20, 32, 45
Shearing sheep 29
South America 12

Sri Lanka 31, 44
Stacks 17, 19
Stooks 16, 17, 20

Thanksgiving 24-7
 First Thanksgiving 24-5
 Thanksgiving Day 24, 25, 26-7
Traditional harvest 16-23, 38-43
 animal harvest 40-41
 end of the harvest 18-19
 forest harvests 5, 38-9
 gleaners 20-21
 harvest-home feast 19, 23
 Harvest Queen 20
 harvest of the sea 42-3
 harvest shout 18-19
 last wagon-load 17, 19
 Lord of the Harvest 19, 20
 reapers 19, 23

United States 16, 24-7, 28, 30, 44
 Thanksgiving *see* Thanksgiving

Acknowledgments

The publisher would like to thank all those who provided pictures on the following pages: ET Archive Ltd. 13, 40; BBC Hulton Picture Library 23; R. Burton/Bruce Coleman Limited 44; Mary Evans Picture Library cover, 18, 20, 22, 35; Sally & Richard Greenhill 15; Sonia Halliday Photographs 36; The Mansell Collection 19, 21; Peter Newark's Western Americana 25; Ann & Bury Peerless 32; PHOTRI 6, 24, 26 photographer B. Kulic, 28, 41; Picturepoint Ltd. 30, 43; Ronald Sheridan's Photo-Library 10, 11, 12; TASS 14, 45; TOPHAM 31 photographer C. Osborne; Malcolm S. Walker 34, 37; ZEFA 27 photographer A. Hubrich, 39 photographer W. Lummer.